THE *It's a* Wonderful Life

TRIVIA BOOK

JIMMY HAWKINS AND PAUL PETERSEN

Crown Publishers, Inc., New York

Published by Crown Publishers, Inc., 201 East 50th Street,
New York, New York 10022. Member of the Crown
Publishing Group.

Random House, Inc. New York, Toronto, London,
Sydney, Auckland

CROWN is a trademark of Crown Publishers, Inc.

Manufactured in the United States of America

Library of Congress Cataloging-in-Publication Data
Hawkins, Jimmy.
The "It's a wonderful life" trivia book / Jimmy Hawkins and
Paul Petersen. — 1st ed.
p. cm.
1. It's a wonderful life (Motion picture)   I. Petersen, Paul.
II. Title.
PN1997.I7583H38   1992
791.43'7—dc20   91-44305
CIP
ISBN 0-517-58787-4
10 9 8 7 6 5 4 3

Dedicated to Frank Capra

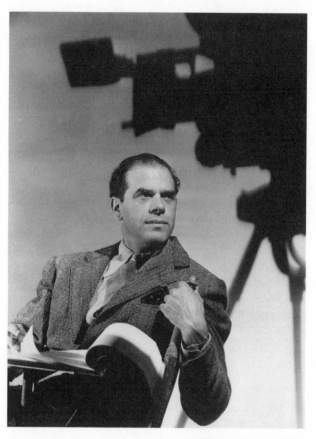

(*Wesleyan Cinema Archives*)

ACKNOWLEDGMENTS

When Seekers of Fact start on their quest they are bound to run into some honestly remarkable people who, as archivists, are keepers of these facts. We are grateful to Jimmy Stewart, the Frank Capra Archives at Wesleyan University and its curator, Jeanine Basinger, and her associate, Leith Johnson; the UCLA Theatre Arts Library, Brigitte Kueppers and Raymond Soto; the Library of the Academy of Motion Pictures Arts and Science; the Donna Reed Foundation in Denison, Iowa; the USC Cinema-Television Library and its assistant Ned Comstock. Our Special Thanks to Grover Asmus, Bud Barnett, and Cinema Collectors, Joseph Biroc, William Blinn, L. Russell Brown, Dianne Cairns, Carol Coombs, Ellen Corby, Mike Donohew, Paul Gleason, Karolyn Grimes, Albert Hackett, Emile Kuri, Bob Lawless, Virginia Patton Moss, Ned Nalle, Esther Newberg, Clem Portman, Volta Music, John Waxman, and Zelma Wilson. Finally, we are deeply indebted to Wilson Henley for his patience and, of course, Betty Prashker for believing. Without their contribution *The **It's a Wonderful Life** Trivia Book* would be a lesser work indeed.

CONTENTS

FOREWORD

*The **It's a Wonderful Life** Trivia Book* is more than just trivia. It was fun reading the question-and-answer portions. In fact, I learned things about the film I never knew. And I was in it. What I found most heartwarming was sharing the letters from other members of the *It's a Wonderful Life* cast and crew. It brought back so many wonderful memories I remember as if it were yesterday. And to know it was written by an actor who actually played my son makes it even more special. From one Jimmy to another, "It's been a wonderful life." I hope all who read this book will enjoy it as much as I did.

JIMMY STEWART

The It's a Wonderful Life Trivia Book

(Donna Reed Foundation)

INTRODUCTION

How well do you know the most beloved movie of all time? You've seen this Christmas classic a dozen times, laughed and cried with its all-star cast, and applauded the director, Frank Capra.

But do you *really* know *It's a Wonderful Life*?

In the following pages you can test your *IAWL* knowledge or, when you're watching with friends, stump them with questions that will make them slap their head and say, "Oh, I knew that."

Now, not all the answers are in the film, but we promise you'll find them in the back of the book. You'll also find a complete cast list and a gallery of vintage photographs. Lots of answers back there. Test yourself before and after you watch this cinema classic.

It's a Wonderful Life trivia makes for a great party game. The book is a welcome stocking stuffer. A present for all generations. Fun for the entire family. Whether you're a casual viewer not yet familiar with this movie or a full-blown film buff, *The It's a Wonderful Life Trivia Book* is for you. There are questions at every level . . . from the novice to the expert. The answers are guaranteed to increase your pleasure as you recall this great film. Some of the answers will surprise and delight you. Some will make you laugh. Most of all, your appreciation of the men and women who participated in the making of *It's a Wonderful Life* will grow immeasurably.

In keeping with the spirit of *IAWL* we want you to know that a portion of the proceeds from this venture have been dedicated to the Donna Reed Foundation for the Performing Arts, headquartered in Donna's hometown, Denison, Iowa.

Well, if we say any more you'll have an advantage. We have answered three questions already. Good luck.

THE CAST

Answers on page 77

Let's get the easy ones out of the way, okay? The answers will get harder as you go along.

1. This actor had already won an Oscar before he played George. Who is he and what movie brought him an Oscar in 1940?

2. Donna Reed played George's wife. She would go on to win an Oscar. What was her character's name before she married George?

3. In what year and in what movie did Donna Reed win her Best Supporting Actress Oscar?

4. This familiar young actor wanted to dance with Mary Hatch. He is best known for his signature role in "Our Gang" (The Little Rascals). Who is he?

5. This actor was brilliant in the role of the villainous rich man in *It's a Wonderful Life.* Who played the mean old man in the wheelchair?

6. Can you name the actress who played Jimmy Stewart's mother?

7. How many times did she play Jimmy Stewart's mother in films?

8. Can you name the little kid who played Tommy? Here's a hint: He went on to play "Tagg Oakley" on television's "Annie Oakley" series.

9. And now a point of personal privilege. How did the authors of this book meet?

10. This actor played the cop in *IAWL.* Who is he and what was his character's name?

11. This same actor went on to star in a classic television western. Name that series.

FADE IN - NIGHT SEQUENCE

SERIES OF SHOTS of various streets and buildings in the town of Bedford Falls, somewhere in New York State. The streets are deserted, and snow is falling. It is Christmas Eve. Over the above scenes we hear voices praying:

> GOWER'S VOICE
> I owe everything to George Bailey.
> Help him, dear Father.

> MARTINI'S VOICE
> Joseph, Jesus and Mary. Help my
> friend Mr. Bailey.

> MRS. BAILEY'S VOICE
> Help my son George tonight.

> BERT'S VOICE
> He never thinks about himself,
> God, that's why he's in trouble.

> ERNIE'S VOICE
> George is a good guy. Give him
> a break, God.

> MARY'S VOICE
> I love him, dear Lord. Watch over
> him tonight.

> JANIE'S VOICE
> Please, God. Something's the
> matter with Daddy.

> ZUZU'S VOICE
> Please bring daddy back.

CAMERA PULLS UP from the Bailey home and travels up through the sky until it is above the falling snow, and moving slowly toward a firmament full of stars. As the camera stops we hear the following heavenly voices talking, and as each voice is heard, one of the stars twinkles brightly:

> FRANKLIN'S VOICE
> Hello, Joseph, trouble?

> JOSEPH'S VOICE
> Looks like we'll have to send
> someone down -- a lot of people
> are asking for help for a man
> named George Bailey.

> (CONTINUED)

Page one of the *It's a Wonderful Life* screenplay. (*Albert Hackett Collection*)

It was such a long time ago. Working on It's a Wonderful Life was great, but the picture owes all its credit to Frank Capra. He had the vision. He saw everything . . . or it wouldn't be there.

We would work together, Frank, my wife, Frances Goodrich, and I. It takes a long time to accumulate things . . . you keep sharing things . . . putting things in . . . pulling things out . . . trying this . . . trying that. It's hard to tell where anything comes from.

Take those first three scripts (from Connelly, Trumbo, and Clifford Odets). We didn't keep a thing from those scripts but a couple of scenes from the Odets effort . . . scenes describing the relationship between the young George and the drugstore man.

Frances and I would write something and turn it in. Frank would go over it with us and then, bit by bit, the story would come around.

Ya' see, the whole thing is like a rag. . . . Everyone wrings you out 'til there's nothing left to tell . . . 'cept what you see there on the screen.

The only thing that matters is how the audience reacts, and what they see on the screen. And what they see is what each person [involved in the filming] brings to the work that makes It's a Wonderful Life what it is.

ALBERT HACKETT
Screenwriter,
It's a Wonderful Life

Albert Hackett lives in New York.

12. He had a pal in *IAWL.* Who as the actor he sang with, and what was the character's name?

13. He had a distinctive job. What was it?

14. This actor also went on to a famous television show. What was the series, and what part did he play?

15. This actor got to play the heavenly role of an angel. Who was the actor, and what was the angel's first name?

16. This female played the highly desirable siren in *It's a Wonderful Life.* Who was the actress, and what was her character's name?

Now, for a few more esoteric cast questions:

17. When the *It's a Wonderful Life* property was first purchased, what actor was considered for the lead role?

18. This man would go on to a successful career as a producer with such credits as "The Danny Thomas Show." Who was he and what part did he play?

19. Jimmy Stewart portrayed the role of George, that you know. What was George's last name in *IAWL?*

20. Jimmy Stewart had a brother in the film. What was the brother's name, and can you name the actor that played the part?

21. The brothers had an uncle. Try to remember his name. Who played the part?

22. The uncle had a crucial failing, central to the movie. What was it?

23. Can you name another classic movie in which this actor had a significant part?

24. Before Donna Reed won the part in *IAWL* another actress was offered the role but turned it down. Who was she?

Thomas Mitchell, right. (*Cinema Collectors*)

It's a Wonderful Withdrawal

During the run on the Bailey Building and Loan I request-ed seventeen dollars. There were many rehearsals and many takes . . . and then Mr. Capra came up to me and whispered in my ear. On the next take I asked for an odd amount . . . not seventeen dollars, but seventeen-fifty. That threw Jimmy Stewart off. He was expecting me to say the amount I had requested in the rehearsals and takes we'd already tried.

But Stewart was wonderful. He ad-libbed his reaction and kiss. That was pure Capra. He knew how to keep things fresh.

ELLEN CORBY
"Mrs. Davis,"
It's a Wonderful Life

Ellen Corby is currently living in a suburb of Los Angeles, California.

19

It's a Wonderful Memory

It was the week of June 13, 1946 . . . right after the war, and people were just getting back to normal. I was a child actor, four and a half years old, going to be five in November. That one-half year was a big deal at the time.

I remember my mom would wake me up real early . . . it was still dark outside. We'd take the bus, then transfer to a streetcar a couple of times (the Red Cars were still operating then). I remember waiting for the streetcar while shop owners were opening for the day. We'd arrive at our destination, the RKO-Pathé Studios in Culver City, right down the street from MGM (We used to refer to it as M-Jim, 'cuz I'd already done a lot of movies there).

We went to Stage 14. When I walked onto the stage, going through the two big doors separated by a little ante-room (and the doors were too big for me to pull open) I can recall the odor. Old soundstages have a peculiar smell. I can only describe it as a cookie smell. I remember that scent, and I remember the nice memory it brings back. People were going around doing whatever it was that they were doing, and I'd go over and check in at the school-room. Then off to wardrobe and after that, a little bit of makeup. Kids don't need much.

It took two weeks to film all the stuff with the kids. I remember Frank Capra getting down in almost a sitting position, a squat really, to discuss with me . . . eye to eye . . . what it was he wanted me to do. He was very patient and would ask if I knew what he meant, and I'd say, "I did."

I remember one scene in particular with Jimmy Stewart where I'm putting tinsel on his head and all of a sudden he grabs me and pulls me into his cheek. We rehearsed this a few times and then did a couple of takes. I was wearing this Santa Claus mask around my neck and every time

The Bailey Family. (*Jimmy Hawkins Collection*)

Jimmy Stewart and Jimmy Hawkins at the *It's a Wonderful Life* picnic. (*Tommie Hawkins*)

Mr. Stewart would pull me to him the rough inside of the mask would scratch my face. I sure didn't like that feeling but I knew enough not to flinch on film. Wow . . . what a trooper.

We finished that movie and waited for the next. I did get together with the cast and crew on August 4, 1946, when our whole family drove way out to Arthur's Ranch. My dad said it was also called Lake Malibu. My brother Tim (my sister Sue hadn't come along yet) and my mom and dad had a great day . . . sack races, spoon races (with eggs), etc. I won the watermelon-eating contest.

Oh yeah, and then they took a picture of everyone from the movie. It was different because we had to hold still while the camera panned the whole group, left to right (over 370 people). The cameraman yelled something during the picture taking and when the picture was sent to us (I still have mine) I knew why he was yelling.

Frank Capra and Jimmy Stewart were standing at both ends!

As the camera panned across the group Capra and Stewart ducked down and ran behind everyone to end up on the other side of the group. Talk about a classic photo!

The whole experience on **It's a Wonderful Life** was just great. It's nice to be part of something that has become a classic. Thanks, Mr. Capra.

JIMMY HAWKINS
"Tommy Bailey,"
It's a Wonderful Life

Jimmy Hawkins is a producer living in Los Angeles, California.

25. This actress needed seventeen-fifty. She had just one line in the movie but would go on to fame in "The Waltons." What was her name?

26. Although he wasn't around too long in *IAWL,* this actor portrayed George's father. Who was he?

27. This actor got drunk and cuffed George on the ear. Do you know this actor's name?

28. What part did the drunk play and what did the character do for a living?

WARMING UP

Answers on page 80

A warm-up for the true film buff: Okay, you've seen *It's a Wonderful Life* a zillion times and you really know films. Try a few of these questions.

1. Can you name the man who wrote the score for *It's a Wonderful Life*?

2. Was his score nominated for an Academy Award?

3. How many other nominations did he garner in his career? Three nominations? Eight nominations? Sixteen nominations?

4. Sam Wainwright was a lifelong friend of George Bailey. What *two* actors played Sam, and what was the character's nickname?

5. Uncle Billy had a pet. This beast appeared in many Capra films. What is it, and can you give it a name?

6. Picture the Bailey family. There's George and Mary. How many kids?

7. Larry Simms, the oldest of the Bailey children, had done many films before *IAWL.* Can you name his other famous family and his character's name?

8. Who are Danny Mummert and Georgie Nokes?

9. *It's a Wonderful Life* started out with another name and in a different form entirely. Here is a three-part question for you experts that will test your superior knowledge. What was the original title? Who wrote the original story? What unusual form did the story have when it first became public?

10. In what year was *It's a Wonderful Life* given its premiere?

11. Approximately 300 movies were released in the 1946–1947 season. Where did *It's a Wonderful Life* rank on the box-office money list? 5th? 27th? 209th?

12. Did *It's a Wonderful Life* make any money in its first release?

13. Which of these three world-class writers tried their hand at writing *It's a Wonderful Life?* Clifford Odets? Dalton Trumbo? Marc Connelly?

Still think you know a lot about this movie? Fear not. You still have plenty of time to show us what you know, you expert you.

It's a Wonderful Set

It's a Wonderful Life is one of my favorite career memories. It is a story of a small town in America; the population was about thirty thousand. A three-block Main Street, the principal set, was built at the RKO ranch in the San Fernando Valley. We first see it when James Stewart, who played George Bailey, is shown as a boy during the 1920s, and then a few years later as he makes plans to attend college. This lapse of years meant that all of the store windows had to reflect those changes. (The neon signs needed to be different, the trees a little taller, and a complete new set of vehicles and houses.) Since both sides of Main Street were shown, there were many more store win-

(*Wesleyan Cinema Archives*)

dows to do over and signs to change from old-fashioned electric to neon.

Then we see the street in the summer of 1943, during World War II, and then in the winter, with snow on the ground and twice with the snow falling. We had special machines to make the snow and rigged the entire set so that the snow could be seen falling naturally. We also had rain sequences and the set was rigged for that as well.

Finally, because of a wish that George Bailey makes, wishing he'd never been born, we see a completely different kind of town; one without Bailey's helpful influence, the man who had helped the townspeople build their lives through the family savings and loan company he took over upon his father's untimely death. It would have been run by a greedy old businessman portrayed by Lionel Barrymore, who wouldn't help anyone, regardless of the situation. Because of his corruption, the town turns into a company town, a brothel town full of saloons, with everybody out for himself. The seed of kindness given the town by George Bailey is completely missing. So this meant yet another complete redoing, in every respect, of Main Street. It required a huge amount of work—so much detail.

Frank Capra was very appreciative of all this fine detail. He never said much, just accepted every set, yet he had a way of speaking to me that made me realize how he felt. It was most gratifying.

Several years later, while filming Rope, *a Hitchcock movie, Jimmy Stewart told me of all the pictures he'd been in,* **It's a Wonderful Life** *was his favorite.*

EMILE KURI
Set Director,
It's a Wonderful Life

Emile Kuri is retired and lives in Westlake, California.

THE STORY

Answers on page 82

You may want to try this section *before* you see the movie again or you might want to test your powers of observation by watching the movie *first*. That's up to you. *It's a Wonderful Life* is a first-rate example of story construction, Hollywood-style.

1. The theme of *IAWL* is consistent from first to last. Clarence explains this theme perfectly. Do you remember what he says?

2. What is the last line of dialogue in the movie?

3. What is the name of the town in which *IAWL* takes place?

4. And where is this town located? In what state?

5. When the movie begins a lot of people are talking. We hear their voices offstage. What are they doing?

6. In what form are the angels Joseph, Franklin, and Clarence first seen?

7. Who supplied the voices of Joseph and Franklin?

8. Clarence is a special kind of angel. What kind?

9. What reward is Clarence hoping for if he is able to help George Bailey?

10. How old is Clarence when we meet him?

11. When we first see George Bailey, how old is he and what is he doing?

12. Here is *true* trivia. What is the name of the kid actor who plays George Bailey as a young boy?

13. What kind of accident happens on the ice?

14. What part of George's body is infected after the rescue?

15. Which one?

16. Where does young George work?

I've said it before. They should give it an Emmy for longevity. It's bigger now because of TV than it was when it was released in the theaters back in 1946. Who'd have ever thought? I was the camera operator on **IAWL** *through the test and worked with two cinematographers, Vic Milner, who left after five weeks and in came Joe Walker (wonderful man). He had to leave after five weeks to do a movie at Columbia. I remember I was sitting on the crane and Capra came up to me—he was grinning from ear to ear— and came right out and asked me, How would you like to take over the picture?*

"Yeah," I said. "That would be wonderful."

"Okay," he said, "it's yours."

That was it. From that moment on I was the cameraman.

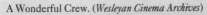

A Wonderful Crew. (*Wesleyan Cinema Archives*)

First thing I shot was the night stuff. In the cemetery— all that snow on the ground! Worst thing in the world to work with. The snow's so bright you can't light it the way it should look with some shadows.

First night there were 120 electricians—and all the gaffer kept grumbling about was "I'm short of men"—I got a laugh out of that. One hundred and twenty guys and he wanted more.

I remember that everyone on the set was jovial. We had a good time—never a dull moment. That's the way Capra wanted it. Capra was generous. He would listen to my ideas, then say, "I think that's fine." **It's a Wonderful Life** was a sensational film to get my start—I was on top. I got screen credit with one of the top cameramen.

With Capra it was always tops!

My first movie as a full-fledged cameraman and it turned out to be the longest-lived one I ever made. It's the one people love and remember.

JOSEPH BIROC
Cameraman,
It's a Wonderful Life

Joseph Biroc lives in Encino, California.

17. Who are the two young girls we meet in the drugstore?

18. One girl asks for candy. What kind and how much?

19. The other girl whispers something in George's bad ear. What does she say?

20. Mr. Gower is drunk when we first see him. Why?

21. Mr. Gower's understandable drunkenness causes him to make a huge mistake. What is that mistake?

22. What is the illness at the Blaine household the capsules are meant to help?

23. How does George get the idea to go to his father for advice about the poison pills?

24. Where does the senior Bailey work, and what is his full name?

25. Uncle Billy doesn't want to let young George into his father's office. But why are we shown a close-up of Uncle Billy's hand?

26. Who is in that tense office with George Bailey's father?

27. How is the senior Bailey supposed to raise $5,000?

28. George goes back to the drugstore with the poison pills still in his pocket. Even though he's beaten about the ear (which starts bleeding), George is able to prevent a tragedy. What promise does he make to Mr. Gower?

29. Does George ever break that promise?

30. When we first see Jimmy Stewart as George Bailey he is trying to buy something. What is he trying to buy?

31. How much is George charged for this purchase?

32. How is George getting to France?

33. On his way home George bumps into two of his friends, Bert the cop, and Ernie the cabdriver. A fourth person joins them. Who is it?

34. What happens to the old man who watches this person walk across the street?

35. Bert is "hot-to-trot" after seeing this person. What does he plan to do immediately?

36. While Pop Bailey is at work, what does Mrs. Bailey do?

37. The Bailey family has a cook. What is the cook's name, and for you trivia buffs, who played the part?

38. When we first see the grown-up Harry, what is he wearing and where is he going?

39. Harry Bailey is chairman of what sort of committee?

40. The scene between George and his father at the dining room table is classic "exposition." Here is a list of things we learn in a very short time. Pick the one item we *don't* hear about.

    a. Potter is now on the board of the Building & Loan Association.

    b. George is going to college.

    c. He was born older, was George.

    d. George wants to build things after college, plan modern cities.

    e. Most of George's friends have finished college.

    f. Mary Hatch is going to be at the high school dance.

    g. George designed the floor of the new gym.

41. Where is the dance being held, and what is the year? What is the occasion?

42. Why does the character named Marty inter-

rupt George as he's talking to Violet? Who played Marty?

43. "Alfalfa" Switzer is talking to Donna Reed when she and Jimmy Stewart "lock eyes." What is Alfalfa talking about?

44. A song is playing as George and Mary start to dance. What is it?

45. Their dance is interrupted by an announcement from Harry onstage. What is Harry accouncing?

46. Many people in 1946 didn't believe that a movable dance floor existed except in the movie, but the floor and the pool were real. Where was this famous scene shot?

47. Speaking of shooting, where was most of *IAWL* shot?

Before we move on to one of the most famous scenes in filmdom, here are a few more "stumpers" in case you haven't had enough.

48. Who played the part of Mr. Partridge, the principal who jumps into the pool?

49. Who played Joe Kepner, the luggage shop owner?

50. Can you name the two young actresses who played Mary and Violet as little girls?

51. What is the gadget George grabs when he "wishes he had a million"?

How'd you do so far? Remember, classic movies are studied word by word and frame by frame. Even the most minor players are carefully noted. The purpose of this chapter . . . beyond an attempt to drive you "bats" . . . is to demonstrate just how remarkable the opening scenes of *It's a Wonderful Life* are. In a very short span of film time we get an extraordinary glimpse of life in an American town, circa 1919 to 1928. We meet all the major characters, absorb their experiences and motivations, learn about their inner relationships, and set the stage for all that follows.

Henry Travers, left. (*Cinema Collectors*)

It's _Not_ a Wonderful Critic

Bosley Crowther, the New York Times:
  "For all its characteristic humors, Mr. Capra's **Wonderful Life** _... is a figment of simple Pollyanna platitudes."_

The New Yorker:
  "So mincing as to border on baby talk ... Henry Travers, God help him, has the job of portraying Mr. Stewart's guardian angel. It must have taken a lot out of him."

The New Republic:
  "Frank Capra (Hollywood's Horatio Alger) fights with more cinematic know-how and zeal than any other director to convince movie audiences that American life is exactly like the Saturday Evening Post _covers of Norman Rockwell."_

The British press was no better. From the Daily Mail:
  "I found the experience more exhausting than uplifting."

(Wesleyan Cinema Archives)

It's a Wonderful Remembrance

My movie career began at age four when mom brought my brother and me down from Canada to get into the movies. She got us an agent, Lola Moore, and we were on our way.

As a youngster, going on interviews was really scary. It was always exciting when chosen, *especially when I was picked to be Janie in* **It's a Wonderful Life.** *The Casting Director thought I most resembled Donna Reed,*

36

who was to be my mother—what a break! Also Jimmy Stewart was to be my dad—Wow! Not having a dad of my own, I got to pretend for a while that he really was my daddy.

Although it was just another job at the time, the most memorable scene for me was while I was practicing "Hark, The Herald Angels Sing," on the piano—I really played it! Mr. Stewart came into the living room very upset and yelling at us all. We were supposed to cry, and believe me it was easy, because he truly scared us—he was so good! I don't believe Mr. Capra had too many retakes of that scene.

Going to school on the stage was fun (maybe that's why I became a school teacher), especially with the kids who played my brothers and sister in the movie. We had to do our assignments but still had time for fun and games. We sure were lucky! My husband, Chet, sometimes tells my students that I played in **It's a Wonderful Life**. They can't get over it. Young and old are really touched by the film. Being a part of it is a memory I'll cherish all my life. God bless!

CAROL COOMBS*
"Janie Bailey"
It's a Wonderful Life

Carol, mother of three, lives with her husband in Crestline, California.

*Coombs was misspelled (Coombes) in the Production Credits—another film flub.

***THE* SCENE**

Answers on page 87

The luminescent Donna Reed in the full flower of her beauty at age twenty-five and the terminally handsome Jimmy Stewart combined with the full measure of Capra's power and cinema magic to create one of the most enduring scenes ever filmed in their stroll down a quiet neighborhood street. Let's see what you can recall.

1. What is George Bailey wearing after falling into the pool?

2. What is on the front of his costume?

3. Is there anything written on Mary Hatch's costume?

4. What are George and Mary carrying?

5. What are George and Mary singing?

6. How old is Mary?

7. What does Mary call the belt on her robe? What does George call it?

8. Mary and George come upon a decrepit house. The house has a name. What is it?

9. Why does George want to throw a rock at the house?

10. What would Mary like to do with the old house?

11. George wishes to: a. leave town; b. see the world; or c. build things?

12. Does Mary ever tell George what she's wished for?

13. What does George *think* Mary wants?

14. Who interrupts this sensual love scene, and who played the part?

Larry Simms, left. (*Cinema Collectors*)

It's a Wonderful Song

My wife, Lisa, and I had been married for eighteen years. The year was 1984. Our eldest daughter was about to enter college. We lived in this great big beautiful house up on a hill in one of north Jersey's more prestigious suburban towns. Our entire world was coming down around us.

The bills became impossible, and the pressure was unbearable. We had two choices: 1. Sell the publishing to all our music, including "Tie a Yellow Ribbon 'round the Old Oak Tree" at a price far less than its true worth. Yes, they can smell it when you need the money. Or 2. Sell our wonderful home and borrow up to our necks. Well, we sold the house and we went from a mansion on a hill to a little rented apartment a couple of miles from the Jersey shore.

That Christmas we bought all our gifts at the one store where we still had credit. The future sure looked bleak, but we decided to "hang in there," and I was going to try to write my way out of the mess.

The only problem was, I couldn't seem to get the next song started, with feeling sorry for myself and all that sort of nonsense. Then one day, just around Christmastime, a movie came on TV we had heard a lot about but had never actually seen. My wife and I watched it together.

Well, we tried to watch it, being two very sentimental fools. Our eyes were glassy for most of that wonderful movie. It was kind of like our own lives. When it ended we felt . . . well, like a renewed spirit. And we had a rekindled faith in ourselves. The message of the movie stayed with us through some pretty rough times that still lay ahead of us.

It's now 1991, and we're about back to where we were at the peak of our success. We still have a way to go, and together we shall overcome life's trials and tribulations. And so I must say . . . It's a wonderful life.

L. RUSSELL BROWN
Songwriter, "Tie a Yellow Ribbon," etc.

15. With George threatening to kiss her Mary darts away. George's foot is on the belt of her robe, which falls away. Where does Mary hide?

16. Is Mary wearing anything?

17. Uncle Billy and Harry suddenly arrive on the scene in a car. What news do they bring?

NO TIME FOR TIME-OUTS

Answers on page 88

1. Who wants to buy the Building & Loan Association when Pop Bailey dies?

2. The association can stay open on one condition. What is that condition?

3. What will George be giving up by staying with the business his father and uncle started?

4. How long has the Building & Loan Association been in business?

5. Two other relatives work at the Building & Loan Association besides George and Uncle Billy. Can you name them?

6. Now name the actors who played these parts. Big points here.

7. What happens to the money George has saved to go to college?

8. What sport does Harry play at college?

9. How do we find out Harry became a "second team All-American"?

10. Have you guessed what actors were the voices for heavenly angels Joseph and Franklin?

11. Where is George thinking of going as he and Uncle Billy wait for the train bringing Harry home?

12. What is Uncle Billy eating as the train arrives?

13. When Harry gets off the train he is alone. True or false?

14. Who is Virginia Patton, and what part did she play in *IAWL*?

15. Harry's father-in-law has a business. Do you remember what kind of business?

16. And where is that business located?

17. Who, besides Harry, has just come home from college?

18. Who urges George to go over to Mary's house?

19. George runs into somebody on the way to Mary's. Whom does he run into?

20. How far is it to Mount Bedford? Five miles? Three miles? Or ten miles?

21. What is the name of the movie theater George passes on his way to Mary's house?

22. Mary, in a teasing mood, accuses George of something as he drags a stick along the picket fence outside her house. What is he accused of?

23. Mary is expecting George. Why?

24. Name the actress who played Mary Hatch's mother.

25. The Hatch house smells like something to George. What is that smell?

26. What song does Mary have playing on the phonograph?

27. To let us know Mary has been thinking of George a drawing is sitting on an easel. What is it and what does it say?

28. George takes the record off the phonograph. True or false?

29. After George storms out he comes back. Why?

30. Who is on the phone for Mary?

31. Mary's mother obviously thinks this person is the guy for her daughter. In fact, he even calls

Mary "his girl." How did Capra let us know this wasn't true?

32. What kind of business does he want George and Mary to invest in?

33. Mary and George are both using the telephone ear piece to listen, which means they are standing very close together. Very close indeed. What does this lead to?

34. And what does that lead to?

35. Who is driving when George and Mary leave town, George or Mary?

36. How much money do the Baileys have to spend?

37. What ruins the Bailey trip?

38. What kind of deal does Henry F. Potter offer to guarantee the Bedford Falls Savings Bank and the shares of the Building & Loan Association?

39. Who comes up with the money to save the Building & Loan?

40. How much money is left after paying off the shareholders of the Building & Loan Association?

41. George has a special name for the money that is left. What does he call it?

42. When Mary calls her new husband home, George heads for the Hatch house. True or false?

43. Mary has devised a "Rube Goldberg" contraption and has the phonograph hooked up to something. What is it?

44. Bert and Ernie serenade the newlyweds. What song do they sing?

45. Speaking of songs, when George enters the Granville house to see Mary a different song is playing. Can you name this tune?

46. Okay, think now: The Baileys are moving Giuseppe Martini's family from their rented house to their newly purchased home. Everyone is piling

Todd Karnes, Virginia Patton, Jimmy Stewart, and Thomas Mitchell. (*Cinema Collectors*)

It's a Wonderful Start

As a teenager, my career choice was to become an actress—a motion picture actress. Living in North Hollywood with my parents (my father was an executive with Lockheed Aircraft), I had been in one or two theater productions in the Los Angeles area. Mr. Capra, after seeing my acting ability, called me into his office with my agent and my father for an interview and subsequently offered me a contract. I became a contract player with Liberty Films, the production company formed by Frank Capra, Samuel Briskin, George Stevens, and William Wyler, releasing through RKO Studio. (I was the only actress ever given a contract by Frank Capra and Liberty films.)

Jimmy Stewart's sister-in-law, Ruth Dakin Bailey, was immediately my first role under that contract—what a vote of confidence for me toward my chosen profession!

In **It's a Wonderful Life** *you first see me at a train station climbing down the train steps to be greeted by George (Jimmy Stewart) and Uncle Billy and being introduced as brother Harry's wife.*

The costume designer for the film had created an ensemble for me—a traveling outfit that included a suit, hat, and white gloves—just the right fashion touch to greet my new brother-in-law.

It was written into the script that Uncle Billy and I, after introductions, were to share a bag of buttered popcorn. What to do about buttery grease on white gloves?

Not wanting to ask questions, I just hoped the camera wouldn't pull into a close-up of my gloved hands. Thank goodness, it didn't!

Still haven't recovered from Jimmy Stewart's big welcoming hug and kiss!

VIRGINIA PATTON MOSS
"Ruth Dakin Bailey,"
It's a Wonderful Life

Virginia Patton Moss is a corporate president living in Ann Arbor, Michigan.

into the Bailey car. How many animals can you recall?

47. Where is the new Martini home located?

48. Here's a tough one. What is the street address of the new Martini home?

49. The house is "toasted" with three things. There is bread, so the house will not know hunger. Salt, so life has flavor. What is the third?

50. Henry F. Potter has a rent collector whose name is Reineman. This character was played by one of the film's most recognizable character actors. Can you recall this actor's name?

51. A sneaky one for the true *IAWL* aficionado. What congressman wants to see Potter?

52. Sam "Hee Haw" Wainwright arrives in Bedford Falls with his new wife. What is her name?

53. Potter tries to buy off George with a three-year contract. How much is George making at the time, and how much does Potter offer?

54. Let's go back to the train station when Harry arrives with his new wife. What song starts to play when Uncle Billy, Harry, and Ruth walk away from George?

55. Speaking of music, what tune is being sung as the Baileys drive the Martinis into Bailey Park?

56. Henry F. Potter has a bodyguard, the guy who pushes his wheelchair. This actor had just one line of dialogue in the film. True or false?

57. Who played the part of the bodyguard?

58. When George returns from hearing Potter's offer Mary has some news for him. What is that news?

59. In what order did the Bailey children arrive?

60. And what are their names? Big points for correct answers here.

61. The Granville house is gradually fixed up, but one thing never seems to get fixed. What is it?

(*The Donna Reed Foundation*)

It's a Wonderful Influence

A wonder is assuredly at its most precious when it's happened upon . . . not fanfared, not hyped, but simply and innocently found. *I saw* Citizen Kane *because it was raining, and the theater on 96th Street happened to be showing it, and I needed to be under a roof until the storm passed. And the storm in the theater was a miracle. Revelation.*

It's a Wonderful Life became known to me in much the same manner. It was late. New York City. Middle fifties. The late show.

What's on . . . ?

And what was on was another miracle . . . a world brand new and yet wholly known. What was on became a kind of shorthand between those who created the film and those who "happened upon" it. Have you ever seen

47

*a film called **It's a Wonderful Life?** And when the response was positive, always enthusiastically so, the two in conversation suddenly had a shared "hometown" and common friends and memories. Uncle Billy was mine and yours and we had danced the Charleston together as the gym floor opened beneath us. We were no longer strangers and it was a miracle.*

Eventually, we all go home again and regardless of what we call it, it's much like Bedford Falls. Whether real or imagined—and what's more real than that which is imagined—it's very much like Bedford Falls.

WILLIAM BLINN
Writer/Producer, "Brian's Song," "Purple Rain," and "Fame"

It's a Wonderful Recovery

*Robert McFarlane, former National Security Advisor, has been very forthright in telling how **It's a Wonderful Life** helped him overcome the depression that stalked him after his failed suicide attempt.*

McFarlane told the New York Times *that his recovery was helped in great measure by finally seeing **IAWL**. He identified strongly with George Bailey.*

*We might wish that Mr. McFarlane had seen **IAWL** before Iran-Contra.*

The arrival of World War II changes everyone's life. Here are some true-and-false questions to see how well you've listened.

62. Mary Bailey joined the Red Cross and sewed. True or false?

63. Mary Bailey ran the USO. True or false?

64. George Bailey didn't join the Army because he was married. True or false?

65. Sam Wainwright made a lot of money during the war making plastic hoods for warplanes. True or false?

66. Henry F. Potter headed the draft board. True or false?

67. Bert the cop was wounded in North Africa and received the Silver Star. True or false?

68. Ernie parachuted into France. True or false?

69. Mary's older brother, Marty, helped to capture a bridge. What bridge?

70. What were George Bailey's jobs during the war?

71. What did George do on VE and VJ days?

72. What did George's little brother Harry do in the Navy?

73. What honor did Harry win in the war?

74. The most pivotal day in George Bailey's life occurred on what special day according to Angel Joseph?

75. When Harry calls George from Washington, D.C., there is a stranger in the offices of the Bailey Building & Loan Association. Who is it?

76. Where is Uncle Billy when George talks to Harry?

77. How much money is Uncle Billy supposed to deposit?

78. Who ends up with the money Uncle Billy loses?

Frankly, I don't remember all that much about working on **It's a Wonderful Life.** *It was, at the time, just a job.*

But I always liked working for Capra. You know I'd done some work for him before: **Can't Take It with You, Arsenic and Old Lace,** *and that* **Mr. Smith Goes to Washington** *feature . . . and when you work with a pro like Capra, you expect the best, of him, the entire company, and yourself, of course.*

There were no surprises doin' that picture. I went in, did my job, and collected my check. Just the way it should be.

'Course it's nice to know **It's a Wonderful Life** *has become a classic. That's a pleasure, sure. But it's always a crapshoot doin' a picture. You get credit for being brilliant when all you did was your job. Ain't that the way? Like missing your golf swing and ending up two feet from the hole.*

CHARLES LANE
Reineman (Mr. Potter's rent collector),
It's a Wonderful Life

Charles Lane is still acting, but he spends a lot of his time chasing golf balls in and around Los Angeles.

It's a Wonderful Sentence

In Florida a few years ago a judge tried to bring a sense of justice to a case involving a man who was charged with the attempted murder of his critically ill wife and who was then going to take his own life.

The judge was struck by the depth of the man's feeling of worthlessness, of his feelings that the world would have been a better place without him.

Thus the judge ordered the man to watch Capra's classic, **It's a Wonderful Life.** Charges were eventually dismissed.

Wonderful Memorabilia

In the midst of this ongoing nostalgia craze it should come as no surprise that **It's a Wonderful Life** *memorabilia has found a niche in the burgeoning market.*

A single lobby poster for **IAWL** *can fetch as much as $1,500 to $4,000 if it's in mint condition.*

The movie's press kit, that collection of studio-supplied artwork in various formats theaters might choose for advertisements, is already worth from $700 to $1,200.

There is also a surprisingly lively market in stills from **It's a Wonderful Life.**

(Cinema Collectors)

79. Are they ever caught, let alone convicted of stealing the money?

80. Getting back to the phone call between George and Harry: Something happens as George Bailey gets on the telephone that film historians consider one of the great film flubs of all time. What is it?

There are many deft touches in *IAWL,* examples of craftsmanship that illustrate the technical skills of old Hollywood. For example:

81. In the opening scene among the stars Clarence is reading a book when he is summoned to meet his superiors. The same book turns up in the final scene. What is it?

82. Animals are often used to imply a benevolent aspect of a character or to invoke sympathy. Now then, you already know that Uncle Billy has a pet raven, but in the scene where George loses his temper with the old man for losing the money, two more animals are introduced. What are they?

83. When a distraught George comes home to the Granville house what song is little Janie playing on the piano?

84. What things did George forget to bring home?

85. What does Pete Bailey want to do?

86. What are Pete and Tommy wearing around their necks?

87. What does little Tommy keep saying to his father? Here's a hint: The expression was later made famous by comedian Steve Martin.

88. What are the two words George is asked to spell by his oldest child?

89. What is wrong with Zuzu?

90. Where does George Bailey put Zuzu's fallen flower petals?

Henry Travers, left; Tom Fadden, center. (*Cinema Collectors*)

It's a Wonderful Fumble

How do you lose the copyright protection of a classic movie? The question is asked over and over again when it comes to **It's a Wonderful Life,** *for the simple fact is that Republic Pictures, in 1973, failed to renew its copyright on Capra's classic. Thus unprotected, the movie could be used by anyone at any time. Is it any wonder that* **IAWL** *is in such wide distribution?*

The saga of **IAWL** *'s copyright history is worth repeating. RKO and Capra's Liberty Films owned the original copyright. In the mid-fifties, a company called M. and A. Alexander purchased the movie, copyright attached. M. and A. Alexander's distribution deal on* **IAWL** *added to its considerable library of two hundred-plus films. This entire library was subsequently sold to an entity called NTA. Later NTA acquired Republic Pictures, whose cor-*

porate identity and name recognition became the name under which NTA operated.

Copyright protection in this era was limited to twenty-seven years. Add twenty-seven years to 1946 and you come up with 1973.

The entity called Republic Pictures had a staff of attorneys, but no one, apparently, was specifically charged with overseeing copyright protection.

Ooops! Call it sloth, or inattention, or extreme malfeasance, but in 1973 the copyright protection of *IAWL* expired. Television programmers across the country took due note and *IAWL* began appearing in every conceivable time slot at holiday time.

There is never a name attached to this failure to retain copyright protection. The explanations use phrases like, "*it fell through the cracks,*" or "*we simply* fumbled *it.*"

And aren't we glad **It's a Wonderful Life** is in the public domain?

91. Whom does George scream at on the phone and blame for Zuzu's illness?

92. What does George do to scare his entire family?

93. When Mary, worried about George, picks up the phone, what number does she call?

94. And whose telephone number is it?

95. Name the young actress who played Janie.

96. Who played the part of Zuzu?

97. Which one of the Bailey children acted in *The Bishop's Wife* with Cary Grant and Loretta Young?

98. What three things does Potter demand as collateral when George comes begging for money?

99. What does George offer as security for the loan he wants from Potter?

100. What does Potter say to George that makes him think of suicide?

101. What is the name of the bar George heads to when he leaves Potter's office?

102. Who punches George in that bar?

103. And who plays the man that punches George Bailey?

104. This actor went on to figure in another bit of Hollywood trivia when he became "the Old Ranger" on TV's "Death Valley Days." Who replaced the man who punched George Bailey as the host of "Death Valley Days"?

105. Remember George hit the tree in his car? Name the actor who played the angry homeowner.

(Wesleyan Cinema Archives)

58

It's a Wonderful Snow Job

I was pulled off the RKO labor gang (group of guys who go from one picture to another on the lot as needed) to report to the RKO Ranch in Encino. It's about a half hour from the Main Lot in Hollywood. My job for the night was to make snow for the Frank Capra movie **It's a Wonderful Life**.

Rumor had it that this movie was special. I was young, early twenties at the time, but as I loaded ice into the machine that sprayed snow all over the street Jimmy Stewart was running down I remember I felt kinda mystic. Of all the films I've worked on, and I've done some great ones, this one seemed to hold out a deep feeling of respect among the crew I worked with.

The story of **It's a Wonderful Life** will endure in the years to come. I feel lucky to have worked on it. I will never forget it.

BOB LAWLESS
Crew Member,
It's a Wonderful Life

Bob Lawless is retired and lives in La Canada, California.

CLARENCE

Answers on page 98

We're about to tackle what most people consider the most memorable part of *It's a Wonderful Life,* the entrance of Clarence the angel. Let's see how memorable the pivotal portion of this film is for you.

1. Here's another chance . . . who did the voices for Joseph and Franklin?

2. Why does George Bailey go into the river?

3. Who is the third person in the first scene with Clarence and George?

4. Do you know who played the part of this third person?

5. What is so unusual about the seventeenth-century sleeping gown that Clarence is wearing as he and George wait for their clothes to dry?

6. Where did Clarence get his nightgown?

7. Big points for the answer to this one. What is Clarence's last name?

8. Here's a teaser for you. When George wishes he'd "never been born," Clarence decides that's a good way to show George what he's worth. Four things happen at once in the toll keeper's shack that tell the audience that things are very different indeed. Can you name two of these events? Can you even name one?

9. What is the name of Bedford Falls now that George has "never been born"?

10. George takes Clarence into Martini's restaurant but the establishment has a new name. What is it?

11. What is the significance of the cash register's ringing bell?

It's a Wonderful Blessing

*Just as in **It's a Wonderful Life,** each of us in some way touches many lives. That makes each of us a special part of destiny. A very special person, Frank Capra, picked me out of many other children to be Zuzu. What a privilege it has been for me to have been part of such an American classic. Because of my involvement I have become something of a celebrity. That has been a really bright spot in my life . . . a life which has had its share of adversity. In order to experience how wonderful things are you have to have some difficult times.*

(Sound familiar? George Bailey didn't exactly say it, but you can guess what he was thinking.)

(Jimmy Hawkins Collection)

The Bailey Family. (*Cinema Collectors*)

My early career and life were affected by the death of my mother, then less than a year later my father also passed away. The Court shipped me to a very small town in Missouri to live with an uncle. I lost all contact with my life in California. Because of the movie, however, local newspapers and TV stations are always running some stories during Christmastime and they mention me. One of these stories was picked up by Associated Press. It was written by my dear friend, John North.

Through that article I got a letter from a man who turned out to be my father's best friend, Perry Vannice. It's been so wonderful (there's that word again) to write and talk with him and get to know about my mother and father.

Another special friend, Doug Moore, found me through the movie. He is a teacher at a local college and a TV critic. He went to a movie festival and met a man named Dale Horning, and Dale had this friend in California who was our neighbor when I was a baby. She knew my parents really well. I have since corresponded with her and found yet another contact with my past.

If it had not been for **It's a Wonderful Life** *they would never have found me. See, "each man's life touches so many other lives that if they weren't around it would leave an awful hole."*

Actually doing the movie left some indelible impressions, and the first one was the snow. I'd been born and raised in Hollywood so I'd never seen snow. Therefore, the winter set for **IAWL** *was fascinating to me. It seemed to me it was like Lux soap flakes floating around with giant fans whipping them to and fro.*

But the thing I remember most during filming was the huge Christmas tree in the Bailey house. It was the biggest tree I'd ever seen, and it was beautifully decorated. It had beaded ornaments. I remember thinking the tree looked like it should be from fairyland. My mother could barely keep me from touching it.

And movie making can be confusing to a child. For example, Zuzu's upstairs bedroom wasn't upstairs at all, but over in the corner of the stage . . . same level.

Bouncing down the stairs (that led up to nothing) on Mr. Stewart's back was really fun. We got to do it again and again.

Since the reemergence of **It's a Wonderful Life,** *some fans started sending me angels . . . as in "every time a bell rings an angel gets its wings." So I started collecting angels.*

Now I look at my angels all year and I am reminded of a part of my life that makes me feel very special. Thank you, **It's a Wonderful Life.**

KAROLYN GRIMES
"Zuzu Bailey,"
It's a Wonderful Life

Karolyn lives with her family in Kansas.

12. Who is the drunk that stumbles into Nick's bar?

13. Why did this drunk spend twenty years in jail?

14. There are a lot of changes in Pottersville. See if you can recall some of the big ones. What has the building that once housed the Bailey business turned into?

15. Who is being arrested outside this joint?

16. Ernie is still driving a cab, but what is different in his life?

17. What address does George want Ernie to take him to?

18. What does Ma Bailey tell George about Uncle Billy?

19. Ernie doesn't live in Bailey Park, but in Potter's Field. What has happened to Bailey Park?

20. When George confronts a tombstone he is well and truly shocked. Whose tombstone is it, and what years are listed?

21. What has become of Mary in this life without George?

22. Where does George go to find Clarence again?

23. After George begs God to let him live again, who is the first person on the scene?

24. What other events occur to let us know we're back in "real time"?

25. When George joyously runs back into Bedford Falls he passes the Bijou Theater. What film is playing there?

26. Can you name the actor who plays Giuseppe Martini?

27. How much money does Sam Wainwright say his office will advance George Bailey?

28. Even the bank examiner makes a contribution to George's rescue fund. True or false?

(*Wesleyan Cinema Archives*)

It's a Wonderful Wife

*Often during my years married to Donna Reed she reflect-
ed on Frank Capra and* It's a Wonderful Life. *The
making of the film was a learning experience. Frank Capra
was a master craftsman and Donna an eager student. She
had already studied acting, lighting, and cinematogra-
phy. From Capra she learned storytelling and the joy of
Americana, whose people were rooted in cultures from*

many different lands. She loved his use of the character actors who portrayed this variety, this diversity of background.

The Capra experience helped Donna to confirm her conviction never to accept the film role of a loser. She saw value in taking on the challenge of a woman who fell on hard times, materially or emotionally, but who rose above the hardship to regain her place in the community.

During the American Film Institute Salute to Frank Capra in March of 1982, Donna was moved when Mr. Capra confided to her that he wished he had made one revision to the film. He would have changed his concept of Mary Hatch had there never been a George Bailey. Capra would have shown Mary Hatch as an attractive, intelligent, and accomplished woman instead of the terrified, weak, "plain Jane" librarian who fled from the advances of the George Bailey she never knew.

As we know, **It's a Wonderful Life** *was not an immediate success. Although Donna did not realize it at the time, some blamed her for the film's failure. Later she had been signed to do another picture and was happy to learn that she would costar again with Jimmy Stewart. She felt they worked well together and looked forward to renewing the association. Understandably, she was surprised to be dropped from the film. The reason given her was that their earlier effort had not been successful and Mr. Stewart was "fighting for his career." It was a hurt that lasted for years, but one which was cured by a "Capra-esque" turn of events.*

For a ceremony honoring Jimmy Stewart, who was turning over his memorabilia to a university, Donna promised to make a contribution. As the event drew near Donna became increasingly concerned about her promise. She did not know what to do, and thus might renege on her promise. Then she thought that if Donna Reed could do nothing for Jimmy Stewart, perhaps Mary Bailey could do something for George. Donna, or rather Mary, sat down and within minutes composed a loving note to George honoring him for his generous gift. Her note was read aloud during the ceremony and was the hit of the evening. Mr. Stewart sent a telegram to Donna (Mary Bailey) thanking her in the name of George.

Donna loved that message just as she loved the "message" of Frank Capra because it reflected what she had learned as a child in the small town of Denison, Iowa. One should honor one's family and one's community. One should give an honest day's work for an honest day's wages. Above all, nothing is more important than the value of a person's word. This was not make-believe created for some film fantasy. Instead it was a credo common to both Donna and Capra—and to millions of other people who know success is worth far more than material wealth.

GROVER W. ASMUS
President, Donna Reed Foundation

29. Name the actor who played the bank examiner.

30. What does the sheriff do with the warrant for George's arrest, and who played the part?

31. What is the *first* song the crowd in George's living room starts singing?

32. Somebody had to contact Sam Wainwright in London. Who was it?

33. Harry left New York in a hurry to get to Bedford Falls. What did he leave?

34. Can you remember Harry's toast to George?

35. Who signed the book that George finds on top of all the money?

36. Way back at the beginning of the movie we hear that Clarence had a job during his time on earth. What was that job?

37. Who is playing the accordion in the final scene?

38. What is the final song of the movie?

39. When the words "The End" come up on the screen what are we looking at?

BRAIN TWISTERS

Answers on page 101

1. You'll like this one. What is the correct name of Main Street in Bedford Falls? We all call it Main Street, but the sharp-eyed viewer might know this answer.

2. The answer to this next question will appear in just a bit. Who is Michael Wilson and what did he have to do with *IAWL*?

3. We have learned that *IAWL* started as a Christmas card. George Bailey had another name in *The Greatest Gift*. Do you know that name?

4. What are the names of the towns surrounding Bedford Falls?

5. Michael Wilson was involved in some great films, *Bridge on the River Kwai* and *The Sandpipers*, to name just two. Does that help?

6. In the famous Charleston dance sequence all the moves were carefully choreographed. Can you name the dance director and his assistant?

7. How many musicians were onstage playing the Charleston?

8. What did Lila Finn have to do with Donna Reed in *IAWL*?

9. Was there a second unit director helping Frank Capra on *IAWL*?

10. Now for some true cruelty. What did M.L. Adams, R.C. Drumm, Kia James, and L.C. O'Leary have to do with *IAWL*?

11. Okay. Who is Michael Wilson?

12. Finally, here's the question to stump even the most ardent *IAWL* fan. Last chance now, who gave voice to the two angels, Joseph and Franklin?

Dimitri Tiomkin's *It's a Wonderful Life* main title score sheet.
(*Permission of Volta Music*)

It's About a Wonderful Score

A beautiful friendship began when Frank Capra hired Dimitri Tiomkin to write the musical score for Lost Horizon. *Together these two men collaborated on six films, including the* Why We Fight *series during World War II.*

Tiomkin's post-war effort on **It's a Wonderful Life** *was a rich and complex orchestration. But before the picture's release the score was completely revamped, much to the distress of Mr. Tiomkin.*

Several of Dimitri Tiomkin's musical "cues" were replaced by Mr. Capra during the final editing process (by works of Roy Webb, Leigh Harline, and Alfred Newman) from the RKO musical library.

The substitution that hurt the most (according to Mr. Tiomkin's musical estate conservator) concerned the film's finale.

Mr. Tiomkin had used Beethoven's "Ode to Joy" from the Ninth Symphony whose literal meaning was "all together we are one."

Capra chose to replace "Ode to Joy" with "Auld Lang Syne," which, from the old Scots and English translation, meant "old times (especially friendships) fondly remembered." Or; "friends remembering friends," a meaning more closely associated with the impact of the final scene in the Bailey home.

These substitutions shattered the friendship between Capra and Tiomkin. They never worked together again.

It's a Wonderful Sound

I have been urging my memory to swing back a mere forty-five years to those wonderful days when I was head of the dubbing (re-recording) crew on **It's a Wonderful Life.** But the anecdotes I might have been able to recall twenty years ago are now gone forever. I do remember this, however: I and my colleagues at the mixing console in the RKO dubbing room knew from the film's first screening that we were about to enjoy the privilege of working on a great motion picture. Its quality was evident in every reel . . . every scene.

As supervising mixer, my specialty was to use the tools of my profession to adjust the levels of the production sound track, correct deviations from normal in the character of the recorded dialogue, and balance the whole in a final mix of the other ingredients: the musical score and added creative sound effects.

Earl Mounce, a former concert violinist, was at second console position and had control of the music tracks. He had been the mixer who recorded the orchestra's rendition of Dimitri Tiomkin's memorable score; now he had the challenge of integrating it into the film in the most effective manner.

Terry Kellum, the third member of our crew, was an experienced sound-effects mixer, capable of manipulating to best advantage the myriad sound effects built into the sound tracks that were under his control.

On the first day of the dubbing session I also remember how Frank Capra and his film editor, William Hornbeck, got the proceedings off to an unusually good start. After introductions and handshakes all around, Capra announced that he would be unable to attend most of the dubbing and that Hornbeck was to act as his surrogate. Then the great man said something that endeared *him to us all: "I've heard about you guys and I look forward to your splendid dubbing job." That's all the incentive we needed, and I don't think we disappointed him.*

I'm sorry to say that Earl and Terry are now deceased. But if they were still with us, there's one thing I'm sure of, they would be as pleased as I am to know that **It's a Wonderful Life** *has not only become a classic but is now regarded by many as the ultimate "American-as-apple-pie" movie of all time.*

CLEM PORTMAN
Dubbing Engineer,
It's a Wonderful Life

Clem Portman is now retired and lives in San Clemente, California.

LIFE AFTER *IT'S A WONDERFUL LIFE*

Answers on page 102

1. How many Oscar nominations did *IAWL* garner?

2. How many Oscars did the movie win?

3. In what categories was *IAWL* nominated?

4. Has the Motion Picture Academy ever awarded *It's a Wonderful Life* anything?

5. Frank Capra received one major award following the release of *IAWL*. What was it?

6. Ward Bond and Frank Faylen became the role models for another famous team on television. Can you name the team and the series?

7. Did the cast and crew of *IAWL* ever get back together after filming was completed?

8. There was a television remake of *IAWL*. Who was the star, and what was the TV movie called?

9. Who played the part of Henry F. Potter in the TV remake?

10. Donna Reed and Jimmy Stewart re-created their roles in a Lux Theater *radio* version of *IAWL*. Who played Clarence in the *radio* version?

11. There is a musical stage version of *IAWL*. True or false?

12. The Family Channel did a movie based on one of *It's a Wonderful Life*'s characters. True or false?

13. Purists insist on watching *IAWL* in black and white. In VHS there are more than 16 options. Bridgestone, VidAmerica (with an intro by Frank Capra, Jr.), Semtar, and Goodtime Video all put out *IAWL*. Video Treasures has the "colorized" version on tape. On laserdisc (black and white) you have, from Voyager, Criterion Edition, a superb laserdisc

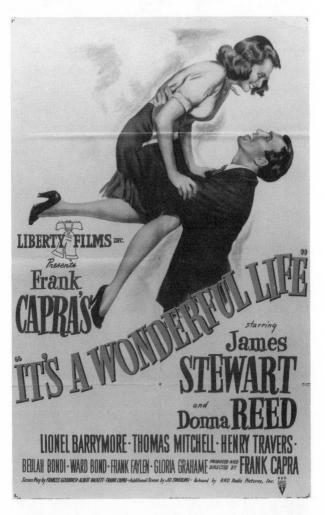

featuring Frank Capra and Joe Walker in interviews, plus theater trailer and photos. Now then, can you name any other products that bear the mark of *It's a Wonderful Life*?

Beulah Bondi and Jimmy Stewart. (*Wesleyan Cinema Archives*)

Brad Johnson, Gail Davis, and Jimmy Hawkins in the "Annie Oakley" series. (*Jimmy Hawkins Collection*)

THE ANSWERS

The Cast

1. Jimmy Stewart. *The Philadelphia Story*.
2. Mary Hatch.
3. 1953. *From Here to Eternity*.
4. Alfalfa Switzer.
5. Lionel Barrymore.
6. Beulah Bondi.
7. Seven times!
8. Jimmy Hawkins.
9. They met while doing "The Donna Reed Show" in 1958 and were still doing the show in 1966. Jimmy Hawkins first played Shelley Fabares's boyfriend Scotty, who later became the friend to Paul Petersen's character of Jeff.

Paul Petersen, Tish Sterling, Janet Langard, and Jimmy Hawkins on "The Donna Reed Show," 1965. (*Paul Petersen Collection*)

Sheldon Leonard, in white. (*Cinema Collectors*)

Frank Faylen, center; Ward Bond, right. (*Wesleyan Cinema Archives*)

10. Ward Bond played Bert.

11. Bond was Major Seth Adams on "Wagon Train."

12. Frank Faylen played Ernie.

13. He was a taxi driver.

14. He played Herbert T. Gillis, the father of "Dobie Gillis."

15. Henry Travers played Clarence.

16. Gloria Grahame portrayed Violet.

17. Cary Grant.

18. Sheldon Leonard. He played Nick the Bartender.

19. George Bailey.

20. Harry was played by Todd Karns.

21. Thomas Mitchell played Uncle Billy.

22. He was absentminded.

Robert Horton and Ward Bond in "Wagon Train." (*House of Gleason*)

Samuel S. Hinds, right. (*Wesleyan Cinema Archives*)

23. Mitchell played Scarlett O'Hara's father in *Gone With the Wind*.

24. Jean Arthur.

25. Ellen Corby had but one line as Mrs. Davis.

26. Pop Bailey was played by Samuel S. Hinds.

27. H.B. Warner.

28. The drunk was Mr. Gower, owner of the drugstore, Gower's Drugs.

Warming Up

1. Dimitri Tiomkin.

2. No.

3. Sixteen nominations for Dimitri Tiomkin in his illustrious career!

4. Frank Albertson was Wainwright as an *adult*. As a *boy* he was played by Ronnie Ralph. Sam's nickname was Hee Haw.

5. A raven. Named Jimmy.

6. Four.

7. Simms was featured in "Blondie," one of the Bumstead kids. He first played Baby Dumpling and the character evolved into Alexander.

8. The actors who played Little Marty and Little Harry respectively.

9. *IAWL* started life called *The Greatest Gift*. It was written by Phillip Van Doren Stern. The writer could not find a publisher from 1938 to 1943, and so *The Greatest Gift* was sent to two hundred people as a Christmas card! The story appeared in *Good Housekeeping* as "The Man Who Never Was" before being published in 1945 as a small book entitled *The Greatest Gift*.

10. 1946. The movie was first shown at a star-studded gala at the Ambassador Hotel, Los Angeles, on December 9, 1946. The New York premiere took place on December 20, 1946, at the Globe, and on December 24 it appeared at the Hollywood Pantages Theater.

11. *IAWL* is ranked 27th out of 300 films released in the 1946–1947 season.

12. Strangely, it did not! Filmed at a cost of $3,300,000, *IAWL* is reported to have lost $500,000 according to Mr. Capra.

13. *All three* turned in drafts of the screenplay. Albert Hackett, Frances Goodrich, and Frank Capra are given credit with additional scenes by Jo Swerling.

Arthur Lake, Penny Singleton, and Larry Simms in *Blondie*. (*Mr. Trivia*)

The Story

1. "Each man's life touches so many other lives, and when he isn't around he leaves an awful hole."

2. George Bailey looks heavenward and says, "Attaboy, Clarence."

3. Bedford Falls.

4. New York State.

5. Praying that George Bailey gets some help.

6. As twinkling stars.

7. Keep guessing, we'll tell you later.

8. An angel, second class.

9. He wants to earn his wings.

10. 292 years old.

11. George is twelve and scooting down a snowy slope while riding a shovel.

12. Bobbie Anderson.

13. George's younger brother falls through the ice and has to be rescued.

14. His ear.

15. The left.

16. Gower's Drugstore.

Bobbie Anderson, Jeanine Ann Roose, and Jean Gale. (*Wesleyan Cinema Archives*)

Thomas Mitchell and Bobbie Anderson. (*Jimmy Hawkins Collection*)

17. Sweet Mary Hatch and the temptress named Violet Bick.

18. 2 cents' worth of shoelaces, which are licorice vines.

19. "George Bailey, I'll love you till the day I die."

20. A telegram has arrived saying that his son has just died of influenza.

21. He puts poison capsules into the package he wants George to deliver.

22. Diphtheria.

23. He spots a Sweet Caporal ad that says, "Ask Dad . . . He knows."

24. "Bailey's Building & Loan Association," and his name is Peter Bailey.

25. To see forget-not strings around Uncle Billy's fingers to show that he is absentminded—an important point later in the tale.

26. Henry F. Potter, and his bodyguard.

27. Foreclose on his loan clients.

28. Never to tell anyone of the mistake.

29. Never. He tells, "not a soul."

Ray Walker, right. (*Wesleyan Cinema Archives*)

Opposite: Alfalfa Switzer, right. (*Cinema Collectors*)

Lillian Randolph and Tim Moore in "Amos 'n' Andy." (*Cinema Collectors*)

30. A large piece of luggage.

31. Nothing. It's been bought by Old Man Gower as a present.

32. He's going to work his way to France on a cattle boat.

33. Violet, now grown into a sultry young woman.

34. He almost gets run down.

35. Go home to his wife.

36. She runs the Bailey Boarding House.

37. Annie is the cook and she was played by Lillian Randolph, who would later star on TV in "Amos and Andy" as Madame Queen.

38. George's tuxedo and Harry is going to a dance.

39. The "eats" committee.

40. Answer: f. No mention is made of Mary Hatch.

41. Bedford Falls High School Graduation Dance, class of 1928.

42. Hal Landon. Marty wants George to dance with his kid sister, Mary.

43. Alfalfa (Freddie) is talking about coming in fourth in a footrace because he was tripped.

44. "Buffalo Gals."

45. A Charleston contest.

46. Beverly Hills High School.

47. The RKO-Pathe Studios in Culver City, California. The lot once belonged to David O. Selznick and was the location of an earlier classic, *Gone With the Wind*. Interiors of the Bailey home were on Stage 14. With exteriors at the RKO Ranch in Encino, California.

48. Harry Holman.

49. Ray Walker.

50. Jean Gale was Mary and Jeanine Ann Roose played Violet.

51. An old-fashioned cigar lighter.

H.B. Warner, right. (*Cinema Collectors*)

(Cinema Collectors)

The Scene

1. An old football uniform, much too big.

2. The number 3.

3. Yes. The initials BFHS (Bedford Falls High School).

4. Their wet clothes.

5. "Buffalo Gals."

6. Eighteen.

7. To Mary, her belt is her train. To George it's her caboose.

8. The Granville house.

9. To break a window so when you make a wish your wish will come true.

10. Live in it.

11. All of the above, and plenty more.

12. Not until they're married. Those were the days of the Hayes Office and the Motion Picture Code.

13. The moon.

(The Donna Reed Foundation)

14. The grumpy man on the porch who shouts, "Why don't you just kiss her instead of talking her to death?" was played by Dick Elliott.

15. In the hydrangea bush.

16. We can only guess about her underthings, or what were called unmentionables then, but the fact is we do see that Mary has her high heels on. There were many ways to get around the Hayes Office.

17. Pop Bailey has had a stroke.

No Time for Time-Outs

1. Henry F. Potter.

2. George Bailey has to become the executive secretary, taking his father's place.

3. College.

4. Twenty-five years.

5. Cousin Tilly and Cousin Eustace.

6. Mary Treen as Tilly and Charles Williams as Eustace.

7. He gives it to his brother, Harry.

8. Football.
9. The voice of the angel tells Clarence.
10. We bet not, but keep guessing.
11. Venezuela and the Yukon.
12. Peanuts.
13. False.
14. Ms. Patton played Ruth Dakin Bailey, Harry's wife.
15. A glass factory.
16. In Buffalo, New York, of course.
17. Mary Hatch.
18. Ma Bailey.

Jimmy Stewart and Thomas Mitchell. (*Wesleyan Cinema Archives*)

Jimmy Stewart and Gloria Grahame. (*Jimmy Hawkins Collection*)

19. Violet Bick (Gloria Grahame).

20. Ten miles.

21. The Bijou.

22. Picketing.

23. His mother called.

24. Sara Edwards.

25. Pine needles.

26. "Buffalo Gals."

27. The caricature has George tossing a rope around the moon and it says, "George lassoes the moon."

28. False. Mary does and breaks the record.

29. He forgot his hat.

30. Sam Wainwright (Hee Haw) from New York.

31. A woman is seen with Sam in his office, kneading his shoulders and playfully teasing him.

32. The same business Dustin Hoffman was advised to get into in *The Graduate*. Plastics.

33. A kiss.

34. Marriage.

Sarah Edwards, left. (*Wesleyan Cinema Archives*)

The Wedding Party. (*The Donna Reed Foundation*)

35. Neither one. Ernie is driving his own taxi.
36. $2,000.
37. A run on the bank and the Building & Loan.
38. Fifty cents on the dollar.
39. Mary, from the honeymoon money.
40. Two dollars.
41. Papa Dollar and Mama Dollar.

42. False. Mary has set up their home in the Granville house.

43. The phonograph is turning a barbecue spit with two small chickens.

44. "I Love You Truly."

45. "Song of the Islands."

46. There are three: two puppies and a goat.

47. Bailey Park.

(*Cinema Collectors*)

Opposite, top: Frank Faylen. (*Cinema Collectors*)

Opposite, bottom: Charles Williams, Mary Treen, Thomas Mitchell, and Jimmy Stewart. (*Cinema Collectors*)

48. 4587.

49. Wine, for joy and prosperity.

50. Charles Lane, a veteran of hundreds of movies.

51. Congressman Blatz.

52. Jane.

53. George is making forty-five dollars a week and Potter offers $20,000 a year!

54. "I Left My Love in Avalon."

55. "O Sole Mio."

56. False. The actor never says a word.

57. Frank Hagney.

58. Mary Bailey is expecting. The expression used is "on the nest," because you couldn't use the word "pregnant" in those days.

59. Boy, girl, girl, boy.

60. Peter, Janie, Zuzu, and Tommy.

61. The ball atop the newel post at the bottom of the bannister.

62. False. Ma Bailey and Mother Hatch did both.

63. True.

64. False. He was 4-F because of his ear.

65. True.

66. True.

67. True.

68. True.

69. The bridge at Remagen.

70. Air Raid Warden. Paper drives. Scrap drives. Rubber drives.

71. He wept and prayed.

72. He flew Navy planes.

73. The Congressional Medal of Honor.

74. The day before Christmas.

75. It's Carter, the bank examiner.

76. He's at the bank.

77. $8,000.

78. Henry F. Potter.

79. Never. This is perhaps the most talked-about factor in the movie. Considering the Hayes Office guidelines in effect in 1946, it's almost unbelievable that Potter gets away with his theft. A movie that stars an angel, however, can reasonably assume some kind of judgment.

Lionel Barrymore, left; Frank Hagney, center. (*Cinema Collectors*)

80. The large Christmas wreath that George has hooked over his arm as he passes out newspapers hailing Harry's Congressional Medal of Honor is very prominently tossed onto a desk just before George takes the phone, but in the very next cut the wreath is still hanging on George's arm. Ahhhh, continuity.

81. *The Adventures of Tom Sawyer.*

82. Look for the little white dog (bottom left on the screen as Uncle Billy slumps in his chair) and notice the sudden appearance of a squirrel that runs up Uncle Billy's arm.

83. "Hark the Herald Angels Sing."

84. His coat and hat, and the Christmas wreath.

85. Stay up until midnight and sing Christmas carols.

86. Santa Claus masks.

87. "Excuse me." Pronounced as "S'cuse me."

88. Frankincense and Hallelujah.

89. She has a cold.

Cary Grant and Karolyn Grimes in *The Bishop's Wife.* (*Karolyn Grimes Collection*)

Bill Edmunds, Jimmy Stewart, and Stanley Andrews. (*Jimmy Hawkins Collection*)

90. In his watch pocket.
91. The teacher, Mrs. Welch.
92. He hurls books and kicks model buildings.
93. Bedford 247.
94. Uncle Billy's.
95. Carol Coombs.
96. Karolyn Grimes.
97. Zuzu—Karolyn Grimes.
98. "Stocks. Bonds. And real estate."
99. His life insurance.
100. "You're worth more dead than alive."
101. Martini's.
102. Mr. Welch.
103. Stanley Andrews.
104. Ronald Reagan, future president of the United States.
105. Farrell MacDonald.

Henry Travers, left. (*Cinema Collectors*)

Clarence

1. It's a brain twister.

2. Bet we caught you here. Most people will say he was trying to commit suicide. Nope. Truth is, George dives into the river to rescue Clarence. Funny how memory works.

3. The bridge's toll keeper.

4. Tom Fadden.

5. Clarence died in it.

6. From his wife on his last birthday.

7. Clarence Oddbody.

8. a. It stops snowing outside; b. George's lip stops bleeding; c. The clothes are suddenly dry; d. George can hear out of his left ear.

9. Pottersville.

10. Nick's.

11. Clarence tells George that "every time you hear a bell ring, it means that some angel's just got his wings."

12. Mr. Gower, the druggist.

13. He poisoned a kid.

14. A dime-a-dance joint called Dreamland.

15. Violet, and we're left to guess why.

16. His wife left him three years before and took his kid.

17. 320 Sycamore, the now-deserted Granville house.

18. He's in an insane asylum since the Bailey Building & Loan failed.

19. It's now a cemetery.

20. It's Harry Bailey's tombstone and the dates are 1911–1919. Because George didn't exist, no one saved Harry and he died beneath the ice.

21. She's a librarian at Pottersville's Public Library and an old maid.

22. He goes back to the bridge.

23. Bert.

Ward Bond, left. (*Wesleyan Cinema Archives*)

24. It starts to snow and George's lip is bleeding again. Zuzu's petals are back, too.

25. "The Bells of St. Mary's."

26. Bill Edmunds.

27. $25,000.

28. True.

29. Charles Halton.

30. Al Bridges plays the sheriff, who tears up the warrant.

31. "Hark the Herald Angels Sing."

32. Mr. Gower, the druggist.

33. His award banquet.

34. "To my big brother, George, the richest man in town."

35. Clarence, of course. He signs with the words, "Dear George, remember no man is a failure who has friends. Thanks for the wings. Love, Clarence."

36. Clarence was a clock maker.

37. Bert, the cop.

38. "Auld Lang Syne."

39. A ringing bell, which was the logo for Liberty Films, Capra's production company. This same bell opens the movie.

Brain Twisters

1. Look for the street sign and you'll see "Genesee Street."

2. Put your thinking cap on.

3. George Pratt.

4. Aspetuck, Kitchawan, Katonah, Chappaqua.

5. That's why they're called brain twisters.

6. George King, dance director. Assistant, Melba Snowden.

7. Eight musicians, plus the bandleader.

8. Lila Finn was the stunt double who actually fell into the swimming pool.

9. Amazingly, the answer is yes. The man's name was Slavko Vorkapich, a Hollywood institution. Slavko literally invented what we call the montage, a series of images used to hurry a story along. The rapid montage sequence after the Baileys settle into the Granville house is the work of Mr. Vorkapich.

10. They were the bit babies, the kids who played the Bailey children as babies.

11. Wilson was a screenwriter, and a good one. He is one of the uncredited writers of *IAWL,* along with Dorothy Parker. According to Mrs. Wilson (and backed up by the Writers Guild), her late husband was working on the unproduced *Look Homeward Angel* screenplay for Frank Capra, who liked his writing and thus gave Wilson a crack at the *IAWL* screenplay. Although his name does not appear on the movie's credits, the Writers Guild—without arbitration, mind you—lists Michael Wilson on *IAWL*'s credits under the heading, "Contribution to Screenplay." What makes this little tidbit so interesting is that Wilson came to Capra on the strength of his writing work on Hopalong Cassidy westerns! Mrs. Wilson

recalled that her husband had no interest in pressing his claim against Frank Capra because he was anxious to get started on *Friendly Persuasion*. Wilson went on to write the screenplay for *A Place in the Sun* and *Planet of the Apes*, to name just two more of his credits. What a wonderful writer.

12. Good story here. Joseph Granby and Maroni Olsen get credit for doing the voices, but earlier William Demarest had recorded the dialogue (on 10/7/46). A month later (11/4/46), Maroni Olsen was brought in to redo Demarest's work. Olsen played the father of the groom in 1950's version of *Father of the Bride*, also written by Albert Hackett and Frances Goodrich.

Life After *It's a Wonderful Life*

1. Five.

2. None. Zip. Zero. *IAWL* was completely shut out.

3. 1. Best Picture; 2. Best Actor (Jimmy Stewart); 3. Best Film Editing (William Hornbeck); 4. Best Sound (John Aalberg); 5. Best Director (Frank Capra).

4. Yes. In 1948, *IAWL* received a Class III Citation of Honorable Mention for technical excellence for the development of movie snow, a mixture of foamite, soap and water blown through a wind machine.

5. A Golden Globe for Best Director.

6. "Sesame Street" stars another Bert and Ernie. Jim Henson was a big fan of *IAWL*.

7. Yes. On August 4, 1946, at Arthur's Ranch for the *IAWL* Picnic.

8. Marlo Thomas starred in "It Happened One Christmas."

9. Orson Welles.

10. Victor Moore.

11. True. Mary Jo Slater produced the musical with book and music by Sheldon Harnick and Joe Raposo of "Sesame Street" fame.

12. True. It was called "Clarence."

13. There are several (besides this book). There is a CD from Telarc (CD 88801). There are two Christmas tree ornaments, one from Heirloom and a Magic Ornament from Hallmark. There is a Christmas cookie tin, popcorn bucket, a collector's plate, and from the Capra Archives at Wesleyan University, the *"It's a Wonderful Life" Book*, by Jeanine Basinger (Knopf). Plus, a high-quality porcelain lighted seventeen-piece Bedford Falls town from R.S.V.P. in Chicago. And it is growing!

Jimmy Stewart and Frank Capra teamed on three different movies: *It's a Wonderful Life, Mr. Smith Goes to Washington,* and *You Can't Take It with You.* Their association has resulted in millions of words in print, not to mention learned television commentary, so we thought we'd share our recollections of Mr. Stewart over the years when, as it happens in Hollywood, we'd bump into each other.

Jimmy Hawkins remembers:

"It was in 1971, on the Warner Brothers lot, when I came across Hal Kanter, who was producing 'The Jimmy Stewart Show.' Hal knew I'd been in *IAWL* and thought it'd be a great surprise if he took me on to the set to meet Mr. Stewart again—after twenty-five years.

"Hal marched me up to Mr. Stewart, who was sitting on one of those long-legged director's chairs. 'Know who this is?' he asked Stewart, who naturally didn't have a clue. Well, it took a few seconds to explain the connection and then we all had a good laugh.

"Of course, the *IAWL* memories started. Now, Jimmy Stewart can spin a yarn—a long yarn. Shooting was delayed because he got into telling us how it felt, just after World War II, to finally get back to work.

"I think the biggest worry for me an' Capra was wondering if we still had *it*, you know, that mysterious *it* that means everything in this town. The war, ya see, had made everyone realize what was really important."

Paul recalls:

"It was in another studio, this time NBC, when I found myself next to Jimmy Stewart, who was wait-

Frank Capra and Jimmy Stewart. (*Wesleyan Cinema Archives*)

ing to appear on 'The Tonight Show.' For five years I supplied the limousine service for Johnny Carson's late-night fixture, and often found myself alone with high-profile celebrities. Fred de Cordova, the producer of 'The Tonight Show,' had directed several Donna Reed shows and when he came down the hall and saw Mr. Stewart with me, he tossed off a funny one-liner about the 'Donna Connection.' That started Stewart into one of his patented rambling monologues.

"As soon as *IAWL* fell into public domain—he told me 'it started showing up all over the place every Christmas, it was like Donna and I had been linked for a thousand years, as husband and wife, or at the very least, good friends, but Donna and I hadn't worked together since Capra put us together. Now, you usually end up friends with the people you work with, but that just didn't happen with me an' Donna. We were aware of each other's careers, sure, but I bet we hadn't said more'n a hundred words to each other since *IAWL*. We really hadn't spent any time together, especially when she started doing her TV show.'

"That link, that 'Donna Connection,' unavoidably put the three of us together at Donna Reed's funeral in January of 1986. After the moving service, which featured Donna's good friend John Raitt singing wondrously, we all ended up in the courtyard of the church, bunched up there because of the demands of the many television news crews who needed their sound bites and video. After that we three had a chance to share our thoughts about Donna Reed.

"Mr. Stewart's remembrance reflected what we all knew to be true: 'Donna Reed was a wonderful gal.' Then he went on to tell us a little tale. 'The casting of Donna was a surprise to me. I got to admit, Capra got me good with Donna Reed as Mary Bailey. She turned out to be the embodiment of goodness, and got me so disconcerted that I kept putting off filming that kiss scene, you know, when we're in that tight two-shot on the telephone? We put off doing that scene for weeks.'

"Many people consider the tension underlying that sequence to be the ultimate in sexual tension, and this in the days before people took their clothes off on screen.

" 'I was so nervous,' Stewart went on. 'There was real electricity in the air. I asked Donna if she wanted to rehearse and she said, "Why don't we just do it?" and Capra, knowing what was going on, agreed. So, there we were, cheek-to-cheek, no rehearsals, hormones out of control, and Capra says, "Action!" Well, we did it in one take. One of the best things I've ever done.'

"The next time circumstances put us together occurred at the lavish birthday party for Jerry Weintraub at Blue Heaven in Malibu, California. We're talking major party here, circus tents, pounds of caviar, Pacific Coast Highway closed down to one lane, more than a thousand people, celebrities all, with Frankie Valli entertaining.

"Jimmy Hawkins spotted Mr. Stewart and his wife, Gloria, talking. The situation was irresistible.

"I walked up behind Mr. Stewart, and just like in the movie started tugging at his coattail saying, 'Excuse me. Excuse me.' He turned around and said, 'Excuse you for what?'

"Let's not start that again," Hawkins said. What a pure show biz encounter. The conversation that followed was really interesting. We got to talking about colorization, especially the colorization of *IAWL.*

"I agree with Mr. Capra," Mr. Stewart said. "This process looks like Easter egg colors were splashed all over the film. There's no shadowing. It looks awful."

During the countless interviews Jimmy Stewart has given over the years he is often asked to name his favorite film. For all his reasons, personal and professional, his response is always the same: *"It's a Wonderful Life,* because it meant so much."

We saw Mr. Stewart again at the Director's Guild Memorial Tribute to Capra on October 26, 1991. "I'll always have a special place in my heart for Frank Capra," said Mr. Stewart at this final farewell. "He is responsible for my career as an actor. Thank you, Frank."

Jimmy Hawkins and Jimmy Stewart at the Frank Capra Memorial Tribute. (*Steve Kiefer*)

It's a Wonderful Sequel

Frank Capra and I had become pen pals springing from his visit to my college's film club in the mid-1970s. In the early 1980s we both discovered that my employer, MCA/Universal, owned remake rights to **It's a Wonderful Life.** *Soon thereafter, he proposed his story for a sequel, loosely entitled* **It's Still a Wonderful Life,** *which he wanted to write and produce but not direct.*

The story found George Bailey facing a second crisis: an estrangement from one of his grown children.

My colleague Charles Engel and I accompanied Mr. Capra to the various pay-TV networks hoping we could get them to underwrite this sequel. Unfortunately, our enthusiasm was not shared by the network programmers, who rejected the new story as "not topical enough" or "not our kind of movie." One cable program executive feared that, "No matter how good it ends up being, not one reviewer will think it's worthy of the first one." Perhaps the latter response explains why this project never progressed further.

Would a Frank Capra-authored sequel ever entertain an audience as much as its progenitor? With Frank Capra gone now, we'll never know.

NED NALLE
Executive Vice President,
Universal Television

Donna Reed. (*Wesleyan Cinema Archives*)

REEL SONS REMEMBER

It happens every year in the month of June—our annual trek to Denison, Iowa, Donna Reed's hometown, for the Donna Reed Festival for the Performing Arts. Grover Asmus, Donna's widower, is always there, as are her children, Penny, Tony, Jr., Tim, and Mary. They wouldn't miss this tribute.

But there's another set of now-grown kids who show up, too. Donna Reed's "reel" children: Shelley Fabares, Paul and Patti Petersen, and Jimmy

Hawkins. The first three were her children on "The Donna Reed Show," and Jimmy played her son "Tommy" in *It's a Wonderful Life* back in 1946. Jimmy also played Shelley's boyfriend for eight years on "The Donna Reed Show."

Time has served to enhance, not diminish, our unique relationships to the extraordinary Donna Reed. She was "Miss Reed" in the beginning, then, by turns, "Mom," "Donna," and finally friend.

Shelley always heads into Iowa first. She is very active in the Donna Reed Foundation, somehow finding time to fit in her costarring role in "Coach," her work with the Alzheimer Foundation, and her life as wife to Mike Farrell. Patti Petersen (now Mirkovich) is the committed mother of two, married to a film editor, Steven, and she usually arrives later. Jimmy and Paul, authors of this book and friends for more than thirty-five years, usually make the trip together. For both of us Iowa is a trip both forward and backward in time.

The ongoing work of the foundation (which provides college scholarships for kids interested in performing arts careers) is the draw of the future, a way to perpetuate the interests and concerns of a woman we both loved. But there is much to look back on.

The mere prospect of walking on the very earth that gave rise to Donna Reed is enough to open the floodgates of memory, and when we met at the airport this year Jimmy told me a story I'd never heard.

"You know," he said to me at the check-in counter, "that I was able to give Donna one of the *IAWL* Christmas tree ornaments before she died, don't you, Paul?"

"You did? When?" I asked, thinking of that gorgeous ornament with the famous portrait of the Bailey family.

"It was on Christmas Day, 1985. Donna had just come home from the hospital and was pretty ill. When I arrived she was sitting in the living room across from a decorated Christmas tree. We talked, and then I told her I had a little surprise for her. I gave her the ornament and when she opened the box that great smile came over her face. She asked me to place it on the tree. I put it next to a bright light where she said she could see it really well. I could tell Donna was tired so I said my farewells. When I leaned down to kiss her good-bye, her soft hand touched my cheek and I flashed back to Mary Bailey's soft hands and gentle nature with me on the set of *IAWL*. Then she thanked me for the thoughtful gift. As Grover walked me to the door I looked back and caught that smile once again—for the last time. Wow! What a special lady."

In flight, I remembered Jimmy's story about meeting Donna Reed again in 1958, when he came on the set to play Shelley's boyfriend on the very first episode.

"You always wonder if someone like Donna Reed will remember you," Jimmy told me. "So I walked up to her, told her who I was, and reminded her that I had played her son Tommy, in *It's a Wonderful Life*. She took my hand and smiled.

"Oh, yes," she said. "And do you remember what we used to call you, Jimmy?"

Hawkins had no idea.

"Rip Van Winkle. You could sleep anywhere, anytime. We had to wake you up before almost every take."

Donna always recalled those kinds of things. On the final morning of her life she worriedly asked Grover to go out to the living room and make sure Shelley's birthday present was ready to be sent out.

Larry Simms, Donna Reed, Jimmy Hawkins, and Carol Coombs.
(*Jimmy Hawkins Collection*)

Grover did as she asked, and when he returned to the bedroom she had slipped away. January 14, 1986.

Going back to the land of Donna's birth has a way of connecting the dots of Donna's life. Her goodness, her common sense, and her notion of loyalty, friendship, and family all took root in that small town of Denison, Crawford County, Iowa. Main Street in Denison looks amazingly like Main Street of Bedford Falls in *It's a Wonderful Life,* and it's changed little since Donna was a girl.

Jimmy and I had to laugh as we remembered the way Donna would talk about her hometown, and especially her Saturdays as a small girl.

"Oh, you would just race through your chores to be free on Saturdays," she told us many times. Donna was the oldest of five children so she had plenty of chores. "Our farm was just outside town so we'd either hitch a ride or walk to Grandma's house in town. Everyone met at the Ritz Theater, of course, for the matinee, just about the best buy in town. Then, if there was any extra money we'd go right next door to the candy shop for some 'vines.' (Just like in the movie.) Then, whoosh, off we'd head for home. Up the stone steps and into the house in time for Saturday supper, excited, satisfied, and incredibly *hungry*."

Omaha is the nearest major airport to Denison, but you have to stop in Denver to change planes to get to Omaha in these days of deregulated air travel. While we changed planes at Stapleton, Jimmy reminded me of that last day of shooting on "The Donna Reed Show" and the wrap party that followed. I told him how well I remember.

I was twenty years old, and after doing the show for eight years a good chunk of my life was coming to an end. All the adults walked up to each other and said, "See you on the next one," but I was certain my life was at an end. How could everyone be so casual? Donna had a pressing appointment with her then-husband, the producer of our show, Tony Owen, but she took time to calm me down, wipe my tears, and reassure me that the future could be as exciting as the past. Jimmy was there, too. It took them four hours to get me off Stage One. I know Donna was late to wherever she was going but she was there for me.

From Omaha you cross the Missouri River at

Council Bluffs and you're in Iowa. My reaction is always the same.

"You know, my entire family is from this area," I'll tell anyone in the van that is taking us to Denison. "We hailed from Cherokee County, just sixty miles from Donna's hometown. Can you imagine what it was like in my family when we found out I was going to be Donna Reed's son? I mean, she was a huge star in our family. An Iowa gal!"

Jimmy never stops me when I get going like this.

Jimmy Hawkins, Donna Reed, and Shelley Fabares. (*Jimmy Hawkins Collection*)

Donna Reed, Paul Petersen, and Patti Petersen. (*Paul Petersen Collection*)

Being from Iowa had nothing to do with my getting the part of Jeff, or course, but my Grandpa Burr took me to work during the pilot and didn't hesitate to introduce himself to Donna. "Name's Burr Jones Luce," he told her, "from Cherokee County. Knew your dad, ol' Mullinger, yes I did." Donna was delighted, even with all the pressure of doing a pilot.

"Bug Juice Luce," she cried, even remembering Grandpa's nickname. And they went off for a visit. Midwesterners love to visit.

"That was the best part of Donna," Jimmy said. "The way she remembered things. Her memory was phenomenal, especially about the contrast she encountered when she got off the train in Los Angeles preparing to go to Los Angeles Community College (LACC). That was something she never forgot."

She had told us many times about the fear she felt in 1938. "I only had my aunt out here," she'd tell us. "And no thought of a career in show business."

Within a year she'd won a LACC beauty contest (just as she'd been named Queen of Denison High School) and came to the attention of talent scouts. "Within two years," she'd recall, "I was under contract to MGM—a naive little girl, really, and virtually unprepared for an actress life."

That's what the Foundation scholarships are all about, providing training and a safety net for those kids from the Midwest who, like Donna, over fifty years ago, still come to Hollywood to seek their fame and fortune. University training, and knowing you have "family" out here, can help ease the transition.

When we arrive in Denison the agenda is always the same. Check into the motel, then rush across the street to Cronk's restaurant for some chow. Cronk's is a landmark in western Iowa. Eric Cronk is a good friend and a wonderful host. The opening conversations are always the same.

How's the family? Got any new pictures? How high's the corn? How's the weather been? You know, the important questions. As soon as we catch up it's off to see my cousin, Bill Mead, and his wife, Cheryl, and their kids who actually live in Denison and have for many years. Bill works for IBP (Iowa Beef), the area's largest employer.

Next morning we go out to the airport for the Donna Reed flight breakfast with tons of food set out in a hangar. Hundreds of people and fresh hot-cakes. There will always be one of Donna's high school classmates there, usually with a story.

"I can see her still," he tells us. "The prettiest little gal in town walking hand in hand with her boyfriend, her first boyfriend. You know, she'd sit on the stone wall across from school."

And Jimmy and I can see the wall. It's still there. It's easy to imagine Donna Belle Mullinger sitting on it, age sixteen, with a future she can't even imagine waiting for her. The wall is on Main Street, the theater just two blocks west and now renamed The Donna Reed Theater.

We'll stop into the Pastimes restaurant and visit with the proprietors, who purchased the furnishings of the candy store we hope to restore next to Donna's theater. Iowans do not dispose of things lightly.

We'll visit with other merchants we've come to know. It's just natural to stop and talk with folks you bump into on the street. There are three hundred volunteers in Denison now. Without them we couldn't function.

We sometimes take one of the guest star instructors and show them the town. We'll stop at the McHenry House, which is now the home of Donna's Academy Award Oscar statue and guarded by the Crawford County Historical Society, then down the road to the highway, where Donna's high school classmates erected a sign in her honor at our first gathering in Iowa. It reads, Denison, Iowa. Home of Donna Reed.

Then east, out of town, to the road that now leads to the country club but once fronted the Mullingers' farm. The road is now called Donna Reed Drive.

The Mullinger Farm burned down some years ago, but the stone steps are still visible. It's so easy to picture the young Donna Reed hurrying up those stone steps after a day in town trying not to be late for dinner. Nothing is lost so long as memory serves.

We do the same thing every year: Get out of the car and walk to those stone steps that used to lead to Donna's front door. We'll pause and reflect, then Jimmy and I will look at each other as if on cue and say: "You know, I'm getting kind of *hungry*."

So it's back down the road and into town for the business of the foundation.

Over the years Donna was asked what her favorite movie was. Her response was always the same:

"Why, *It's a Wonderful Life,* of course."

". . . of course."

FRANK CAPRA'S
"It's a Wonderful Life"
JAMES STEWART and DONNA REED

LIBERTY FILMS

'Twas Wonderful Fun

When this book project started we had no idea how much fun we'd have doing the research. Tracking down and reaching out to the surviving participants of **It's a Wonderful Life** provided our brightest moments. We hope you've enjoyed their testimonials as much as we enjoyed finding old friends.

When we reached the screenwriter, Albert Hackett, his wife informed us he was out shopping on New York City's West Side, which he does almost every day—and this when he's well into his nineties. We had to talk the actor Charles Lane off the golf course to have a few words. The lady who helped with Karolyn Grimes's typing told her an amusing tale. Seems she owns just one videotape, and that's **It's a Wonderful Life.** The kicker is that she doesn't own a VCR, but she has that tape.

We spoke with Larry Simms (Peter Bailey) who now lives with his family in the state of Washington. He reminisced with us about **IAWL** and that he had the most fun *spending his spare time talking with the technicians on the set. His curiosity for this led him into the specialized field of communications, which takes him all over the world.*

We caught up with Bobbie Anderson, who lives in the San Fernando Valley with his wife Victoria, as he was literally walking out the door to catch a plane for a motion picture location. He told us he met with Frank Capra three or four times and even tested for IAWL before signing on to play the part of Little George. Bobbie stayed in the industry working in production. He has some great credits on the other side of the camera, too.

We discovered that the IAWL still photographer, Gaston Longet, is almost never given credit. Well, we've just corrected that oversight.

The business end of It's a Wonderful Life was completely fascinating. Did you know that the many companies that produce the IAWL video have a combined annual sales of 600,000 copies? The movie has been dubbed in several languages.

We asked cameraman Joe Biroc what he thought of colorization, figuring he'd have the same opinion as Jimmy Stewart (who doesn't like it). Joe surprised us when he said, "If color means more people watch the movie, then I'm for it." That sentiment has also been expressed by Jimmy Hawkins, who said, in US magazine, "They could put it in polka dots. It's the message that counts."

The original purpose of this effort was to provide the basis for a parlor game at Christmastime, when It's a Wonderful Life is all over the airwaves and people throw IAWL parties. We left the scoring system up to you. We had several trial runs with friends and family and wore out a couple of videotapes—and had a lot of laughs along the way. You'd be amazed how often the authors were left scrambling for an answer.

The simple Q-and-A format gradually gave way to what we hope is a more rounded presentation. The let-

ters will never lose their special meaning, and many of the photographs have never before appeared in print. We finally decided this book should be a keepsake in and of itself, something you pack with the Christmas ornaments and bring out when the Christmas season rolls around.

Of one thing we're certain. We did not discover every last thing about **It's a Wonderful Life**. Many of our readers have answers to questions we never thought to ask and personal stories that turn on the message of the movie. We'd love to hear from you.

It's our sincerest hope that you get as much pleasure from this book as we found putting it together. Thanks for stopping in.

See ya next year.

JIMMY HAWKINS
PAUL PETERSEN

FILM CREDITS

Cast

George Bailey	Jimmy Stewart
Mary Hatch Bailey	Donna Reed
Henry F. Potter	Lionel Barrymore
Ma Bailey	Beulah Bondi
Uncle Billy	Thomas Mitchell
Clarence	Henry Travers
Ernie	Frank Faylen
Bert	Ward Bond
Violet Bick	Gloria Grahame
Mr. Gower	H.B. Warner
Harry Bailey	Todd Karns
Pop Bailey	Samuel S. Hinds
Cousin Tillie	Mary Treen
Sam "Hee Haw" Wainwright	Frank Albertson
Ruth Dakin Bailey	Virginia Patton
Peter Bailey	Larry Simms
Janie Bailey	Carol Coombs
Zuzu Bailey	Karolyn Grimes
Tommy Bailey	Jimmy Hawkins
Freddie	Alfalfa Switzer
Cousin Eustace	Charles Williams
Mr Martini	Bill Edmonds
Mrs. Martini	Argentina Brunetti
Annie	Lillian Randolph
Little George	Bobbie Anderson
Little Sam	Ronnie Ralph
Little Mary	Jean Gale
Little Violet	Jeanine Ann Roose
Little Marty	Danny Mummert
Little Harry	Georgie Nokes
Nick the Bartender	Sheldon Leonard
Bodyguard	Frank Hagney
Rent Collector (Reineman)	Charles Lane
Tom (at Building & Loan)	Edward Kean

Mr. Partridge	Harry Holman
Hal Landon	Marty Hatch
Mickey (with Alfalfa)	Bobby Scott
Dr. Campbell	Harry Cheshire
Bank Examiner	Charles Halton
Bank Teller	Ed Featherstone
House Owner	Farrell Macdonald
Tollhouse Keeper	Tom Fadden
Bill Poster	Gary Owen
Mr. Welch	Stanley Andrews
Jane Wainwright	Marian Carr
Man on Porch	Dick Elliott
Mrs. Davis (Building & Loan)	Ellen Corby
Sheriff	Al Bridges

Technical

Producer-Director	Frank Capra
Writers	Frances Goodrich
	Albert Hackett
	Frank Capra
Additional Scenes	Jo Swerling
Film Editor	William Hornbeck
Photography	Joe Walker
	Joseph Biroc
Special Effects	Russell Cully
Art Direction	Jack Okey
Set Decorator	Emile Kuri
Makeup	Gordon Bau
Costumes	Edward Stevenson
Assistant Director	Arthur S. Black
Sound	John Aalberg
	Richard Van Hassen
	Clem Portman

R K O RADIO PICTURES, INC.

Call Sheet

Date **TUES. 6/25/46**

Director **Frank Capra**

PRODUCTION NO. **541** TITLE **IT'S A WONDERFUL LIFE** COMPANY CALL **9 am**

NAME	TIME	LOCATION — STAGE — SET — COSTUMES, ETC.
MADEUP READY TO WORK		**INT. & EXT. OF GEO'S. & MARY'S HOME**
James Stewart	9:00 am	
Donna Reed	"	**SET 40 - PATHE STAGE 14**
Larry Sims	"	
Carol Coomes	"	So. 171 through 182
Karolyn Grimes	"	
Jimmy Hawkins	"	**TODAY'S REQUIREMENTS**
Chas. Halton	"	
Thos. Mitchell	"	**CAMERA DEPT.** **WARDROBE DEPT.**
H. B. Warner	"	2 Cameras 1 Wardrobe Woman
Frank Faylen	"	3 Assistants 2 Wardrobe Men
Ward Bond	"	2 Operators
Gloria Grahame	"	1 Stillman
Beulah Bondi	"	
Sara Edwards	"	**SOUND DEPT.**
Bill Edmonds	"	Mixer
Mary Treen	"	2 Boommen
Chas. Williams	"	4 Cablemen
Frank Hagney	"	PA & Operator
L. Randolph	"	1 Recorder
BITS & EXTRAS as req.	"	
		ELECTRIC DEPT.
STANDINS:		Best boy and 12 Elec.
Duke McGrath	8:00 am	
Francis Haldorn	"	**PROPERTY DEPT.**
Henry Stone	"	2 Propmen
Luz Potter	"	Greenman
Nels Nelson	"	
1 for H. B. Warner	"	**MAKEUP DEPT.**
1 for Ward Bond	"	2 Makeup Men
1 for Beulah Bondi	"	2 Hairdressers
1 for L. Randolph	"	
1 for Chas. Williams	"	**LABOR DEPT.**
1 for Thos. Mitchell	"	2 Laborers
TRANSPORTATION:		
John Coon		**GRIP DEPT.**
2 Sedans - Lv.	7:30 am	Best boy and 8 grips
SPECIAL EFFECTS:		**MUSIC DEPT.**
4 Spec. Eff. men		1 Standby piano player
(Wind machine & Opr.)		1 Standby accordian player
(Blower & Operator)		
(Snow machine & Opr.)		STAFF & CREW (Report to Pathe)
PAINT DEPT:		READY TO SHOOT - 9:00 am
2 Standby painters		
HAROLD MINNEAR:		Art Black (HT)
1 Welfare Worker		ASSISTANT DIRECTOR

DAY	DATE	DESCRIPTION OF SET OR LOCATION	ACTOR'S NUMBER	SET No.	LOCATION OR STUDIO	DAY OR NITE
Wed.	6-26	Int. George's Living Rm. - Christmas - 1945 - Finale	1-2-4-6-7-8-11-12- 13-14-15-16-18-25- 26-B-X's	40	Pathe 14	N
Thur.	6-27	Ext. Geo. & Mary's home.	1-2-5-B-X's	15-40	Ranch	N
Fri.	6-28	Ext. Potter's Window	1-5-B-X's	15	"	N
		" " Office window	1-5-B-X's	15	"	D
		" " Window	5	15	"	D
		" " Office	1-5-10	15	"	N

It's a Wonderful Cast. (*Jimmy Hawkins Collection*)

It's a Wonderful New Audience, Comrade

The Daily Variety *reported "The first Russian airing of the Capra classic* **It's a Wonderful Life** *will be shown New Year's Day, 1992, the first official day of the nation's new 'commonwealth' status."*

Ain't that somethin'? This was all made possible by the American Spirit Foundation, whose president, Peter F. Paul, explained, "Hopefully, the uplifting and inspirational nature of the film will help the Russian people persevere through the hardships they are facing."

It's a Wonderful Life *will be introduced with a special greeting (translated) from the film's star, Jimmy Stewart, and shown throughout the new nation . . . with the exception of the Republic of Georgia.*

IF IT'S TRUE, that nations are built through decency, endurance, and the kindness of individuals, then we couldn't send a better example than **It's a Wonderful Life.**